TIME FOR KIDS READERS

ATLANTA

by John Allen Hudson

Harcourt

Orlando   Austin   Chicago   New York   Toronto   London   San Diego

Visit *The Learning Site!*
www.harcourtschool.com

An old saying goes that no matter where in the world you travel, you will probably have to change planes in Atlanta. It's meant as a joke, of course. It's true, though, that Atlanta, Georgia, has one of the world's busiest airports. Most of the people who pass through that airport are switching planes, on their way to someplace else.

It's too bad all those people just rush through without stopping. They're missing a place well worth visiting. Atlanta is a city of more than 400,000 people. It has a population of 3 million more in the surrounding area.

Atlanta lies in northern Georgia, in the foothills of the Blue Ridge Mountains. The area is known for its rolling hills and wonderful canopy of trees. The city of Atlanta itself is relatively small at just 132 square miles (342 sq km). Its wider area, however, covers a much greater expanse—6,126 square miles (15,866 sq km), spread over 20 counties. Almost 40 percent of Georgia's entire population lives within this metro area. Most people live in five counties: Clayton, Cobb, DeKalb, Fulton, and Gwinnett.

Hartsfield Atlanta International Airport is a very busy place!

UNITED STATES

Atlanta

Georgia

Atlanta, Georgia, is the city with the largest
population in the southeastern United States.

The historic heart of downtown Atlanta is called *Five Points*. Five Points is surrounded by modern office towers and midrise buildings. The city's largest commuter train station can be found there. It's also home to Underground Atlanta. That's a huge shopping and entertainment section lying just below street level.

Atlanta is famous for its older neighborhoods. They have block after block of large houses, curving streets, and towering trees. Here, visitors find Grant Park. It's home to the city's zoo. Druid Hills, a development, is there, too. It was planned by Frederick Law Olmstead. He was a world-famous landscape architect.

Atlantans find time to relax by a fountain.

Over the years, many of Atlanta's citizens have played big roles in society and in politics. Jimmy Carter, the thirty-ninth President of the United States is from Atlanta. So was Dr. Martin Luther King, Jr., the civil rights leader.

Learning more about Atlanta is never a problem for visitors. Atlantans are always eager to share information about their city with newcomers. Boosterism, telling everyone within earshot why you've got something great, is more than a common trait in Atlanta. It is a civic virtue.

People have always traveled though Atlanta. After all, the community started out as a railroad stop. In 1837, the Western and Atlantic Railroad needed a town for the end of a new rail line. So the company established a community called *Terminus*. In 1843, the town was renamed Marthasville, after the daughter of the governor of the state of Georgia. Less than two years later, the citizens grew tired of that name, too. A railroad engineer named J. Edgar Thompson suggested the name Atlanta. The funny thing is, no one seems to be sure where the name came from. Some people say it's a version of the "Atlantic" in Western and Atlantic Railroad. Others say it comes from Atlantis, the name of a legendary lost continent.

Whichever story you choose, the name stuck—and the city of Atlanta grew. Within 20 years after it was founded, Atlanta had become known as the Gate City of the South. Its location near the southern part of the east coast and at the southern end of the Appalachian Mountains made it a crossroads for the growing nation. With four intersecting train lines running in and out of the city, it was easy to transport goods and people from north to south and back again.

A photo taken about 1880 shows trains carrying cotton north from Atlanta.

It wasn't long before Atlanta was a part of another nation: the Confederate States of America. By 1861, eleven southern states, including Georgia, had broken away from the rest of the United States and formed their own government. War between the Union and the Confederacy soon followed.

By 1864, Atlanta's role as a railroad and industrial center made the city a valuable prize to General Ulysses S. Grant, commander of the Union Army. Grant knew that if he captured Atlanta, it would be nearly impossible for Confederate armies to receive supplies and more troops. So in the spring of 1864, Grant sent General William T. Sherman's army into Georgia.

Confederate forces won the Battle of Kennesaw Mountain in 1864, allowing them to protect—for a short time—the railroad lines linked to Atlanta.

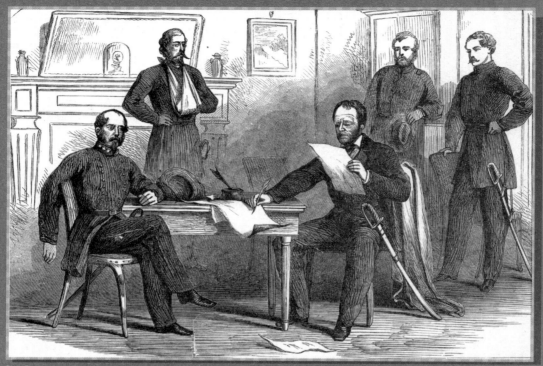

Confederate General Joseph E. Johnston surrenders his troops to Union General William T. Sherman.

The Confederates fought Sherman all the way from Chattanooga, Tennessee, to Atlanta. By August of 1864, though, Sherman had Atlanta surrounded. All during that long, hot month, tons of artillery shells were shot into the city. One by one, he cut the railroads linking Atlanta with the rest of the South. Finally, on September 2, 1864, Sherman and his troops took possession of Atlanta. "Atlanta is ours, and fairly won," he telegraphed his bosses in Washington, D.C.

Sherman's army occupied the city for a few months. Then, before moving on to Savannah, about 250 miles (402 km) away, the army burned Atlanta to the ground. Sherman's object, he said, was to "make Georgia howl.". He wanted to make sure that Southerners could never again wage war. Historians still debate what Sherman did. Some say his actions were too harsh. Sherman justified himself in a letter to Atlanta's mayor, saying, "We don't want . . . anything you have, but we do want and will have a just obedience to the laws of the United States. That we will have, and if it involved the destruction of your improvements, we cannot help it."

After retiring from the Army, popular war hero William Tecumseh Sherman refused to become a candidate for President. He said, "If nominated I will not accept. If elected, I will not serve."

Once the Civil War ended in 1865, Atlanta's citizens quickly set about rebuilding their city. By 1900, it was once again an important manufacturing and retailing center. It had nearly 90,000 residents.

Over the next century, Atlanta grew even bigger and busier, as industry led the way. Today's Atlanta is the center for many of the nation's transportation and communication industries. For example, Hartsfield Atlanta International Airport, south of the city limits, ranks as the world's busiest airport. A major airline, Delta, has its main offices in Atlanta, as does United Parcel Service (UPS), the largest U.S. package delivery company. Two important communications companies are based in Atlanta. They are Cable News Network (CNN) and Bell South. Several daily newspapers serve the area. Not surprisingly, Atlanta is still the major railroad center for the southeastern United States.

Since 1868, Atlanta has been the capital city of the state of Georgia. Many state and federal government offices and agencies can be found here. Atlanta is also home to the region's Federal Reserve Bank. It is responsible for putting new money into circulation. It also removes old, worn-out bills.

Recent developments have taken place far outside the city's limits. Big shopping malls are now found in the suburbs. Most are surrounded by businesses. Office buildings there draw more customers than those located downtown.

All this growth is perhaps the source of one of Atlanta's biggest headaches—getting around. The city's public transportation system, Metropolitan Atlanta Rapid Transit Authority (MARTA), links the city with bus and train routes. However, locations are so spread out that many people need a car to get from one place to another. The area is served by three interstate highways and is surrounded by a fourth. Four-lane and six-lane highways lead in all directions. Traffic is a constant complaint. It's not unusual for drivers to spend an hour or two each morning stuck in slow traffic on their way to work.

Many Atlantans drive long distances to and from work each day.

The Georgia state capitol is located in Atlanta.

Since the time of the Civil War, Atlanta has been known as a diverse city. For nearly 150 years, African Americans have made up at least one-third of Atlanta's population. Today, a majority of the people who live in the city—about 61 percent—are African Americans.

Things were sometimes difficult for Atlanta's minorities. In 1906, a race riot erupted in the city. Tension between white residents and African Americans continued to grow for several decades. As a result, African American businesses moved away from the central business district. They went to an area near Auburn Avenue. Auburn Avenue gradually became an important street. It is known across the country for its African American businesses and churches.

As the years went on, however, business, industry, and growth overcame racism. In the late 1960s, the city peacefully integrated its schools with white and African American children attending the same schools. Maynard Jackson became the first African American mayor of a major southern city when he became mayor of Atlanta in 1973. Of course, Atlanta's own Dr. Martin Luther King, Jr., has earned a place in history because of his devotion to nonviolent protests during the Civil Rights movement.

King's home and his tomb in Atlanta are part of the Martin Luther King, Jr., National Historic Site.

Three historically African American colleges—Clark Atlanta University, Morehouse College, and Spelman College—are located in Atlanta.

It's probably impossible to write about Atlanta without mentioning *Gone with the Wind*, a thousand-page novel written by Atlanta's own Margaret Mitchell. Published in 1936, the story of one woman's fight to protect herself and her home during the Civil War remains one of the most popular books ever written. More than 28 million copies have been sold in more than 37 countries. In 1939, a movie based on the novel had its premiere in Atlanta. The film version of *Gone with the Wind* won eight Academy Awards, including the Best Picture award. The movie left the city forever linked in the minds of audiences with the novel's characters and its depiction of the burning of Atlanta.

Margaret Mitchell isn't the only famous writer Atlanta has produced, though. Joel Chandler Harris, who lived in the late 1800s and early 1900s, was as famous in his time as Margaret Mitchell was in hers. His Uncle Remus tales were based on a series of fables he'd heard in his childhood from former slaves. The books were written in their dialect. Translated into 27 languages, these stories gave readers worldwide an appreciation of tales that had their origins in Africa.

A giant sign in Times Square in New York advertises the opening of *Gone with the Wind*.

Clark Gable and Vivien Leigh starred in the movie version of Margaret Mitchell's novel.

Atlanta is like every other U.S. city in one respect—children have to go to school! The Atlanta area's 700 public schools serve about 500,000 students. The largest school system in the area is in Gwinnett County. Not all children are enrolled in public school, however. About 36,000 students attend the 185 church-supported and other private schools in the area.

The state of Georgia has a program called the Helping Outstanding Pupils Educationally (HOPE) Scholarship. It guarantees any Georgia student who graduates with at least a B average free tuition at any public state college or university and partial tuition at any private state school. Atlanta has about 35 colleges and universities that are available in addition to others statewide, so the choice is wide and varied.

Clark Atlanta University students walk across the school's campus.

Emory University was founded in 1837. It has been located in Atlanta since 1919.

TFK QUOTES

What Kids Say

We asked some Atlantan fifth graders to tell us what they like most and what they like least about their city.

"What I like the best is if you need a job, you can get a job. What's worst is if you have a job you will be late because of traffic."
— *Megan M.*

"What I like best is the great Braves games. What I don't like about Atlanta is we do not have a big amusement park."
— *Richard B.*

"The best thing about Atlanta is the stores. The worst thing about Atlanta is the traffic at the malls."
— *Megan S.*

"The best thing is people are friendly, so it's easy to make friends."
— *Mitchell D.*

"The best thing about Atlanta is getting to go to the Braves baseball games. It's also the worst thing because every time I go they lose."
— *Lindsey P.*

Like any big, modern city, Atlanta has its share of great museums and libraries that appeal to children and grownups alike. The many cultural attractions include the Robert W. Woodruff Arts Center, which houses the Alliance Theater. The Atlanta Symphony Orchestra and the High Museum of Art are also enjoyed by Atlantans. The Michael C. Carols Museum at Emory University tops the lists of popular museums in the city. The Carols Museum recently added a collection of ancient Egyptian mummies and coffins. Most of the money to pay for the exhibit was donated by area schoolchildren.

Atlanta has other kinds of museums as well. The Fern Bank Science Center, for example, boasts a planetarium, a theater, a forest preserve, and

A giant mobile titled *Three Up, Three Down* by American artist Alexander Calder stands outside the High Museum of Art.

Water lilies float at the Atlanta Botanical Garden.

many exhibits. The Atlanta Historical Society features a re-created farmstead from the 1800s, a museum, and a library of local history. The Atlanta Botanical Garden, set in Piedmont Park (the city's most popular park), is nationally famous for its two-acre Children's Garden. It has a three-story tree house. The Carter Presidential Center houses the Jimmy Carter Library and the Carter Center of Emory University.

Atlantans have always loved big events. So it seems only natural that many major sports teams would find a home here. Atlanta's five major league sports teams—hockey's Thrashers, football's Falcons, baseball's Braves, soccer's Magic, and basketball's Hawks—are always able to find a hometown crowd to cheer them on.

Atlanta's athletes have set their fair share of records, too. In 1974, Hank Aaron broke the career home run record set four decades earlier by Babe Ruth. Many of Atlanta's school kids took the day off to join the downtown parade that celebrated the Braves' victory in the 1995 World Series. In 1999, the Atlanta Falcons made it all the way to the Super Bowl.

In 1996, Atlanta hosted the Centennial Olympic Games. They marked the one hundredth anniversary of the first modern Olympics. The city spent years preparing to host athletes and officials from 197 nations. Two new sports, softball and women's soccer, were played for the first time at the Atlanta Olympic Games. Teams from the United States won gold medals in both sports.

When the International Olympic Committee awarded the city the 1996 Summer Games, Atlanta presented itself as a destination to be seen. While many people merely "pass through," others are finding it historically and culturally rich. Thanks to companies that got started in Atlanta and have stayed there, many others have been encouraged to do the same. Atlanta truly has lots to offer visitors and residents alike.

Athletes in the 1,500 meter (4,921 ft) run competed in the Olympic Games that were held in Atlanta in 1996.

TFK

WHAT YOU'LL FIND IN ATLANTA

CNN
When it comes to TV news, Atlanta is the place to be! The Cable News Network (CNN) started in 1980, and its studios are located there.

Coca-Cola
In 1886, an Atlanta pharmacist invented a sweet syrup for a soft drink, Coca-Cola. More than 100 years later, that syrup is still the basis of Coca-Cola and the company still has its headquarters in Atlanta.

Pandas
Zoo Atlanta has a set of giant pandas, Lun Lun and Yang Yang.

Center for Puppetry Arts
Built in 1978 (Kermit the Frog cut the opening-day ribbon!), this is one of the only museums in the United States devoted to the history and practice of puppetry.

U.S. Centers for Disease Control and Prevention (CDC)
The CDC is the federal government's primary agency for researching some of the world's most fearsome diseases. It maintains its headquarters just outside the city limits and has many nearby laboratories.

Giant Chinese panda Yang Yang searches for some bamboo to eat at Zoo Atlanta.